STONE CIRCLE STORIES: CULTURE AND FOLKTALES

ADVENTURE STORIES

BY VIRGINIA LOH-HAGAN

People have been telling stories since the beginning of time. This series focuses on stories found across cultures. You may have heard these stories from your parents or grandparents. Or you may have told one yourself around a campfire. Stories explain the world around us. They inspire. They motivate. They even scare! We tell stories to share our history.

45th Parallel Press

Published in the United States of America by Cherry Lake Publishing
Ann Arbor, Michigan
www.cherrylakepublishing.com

Reading Adviser: Marla Conn MS, Ed., Literacy specialist, Read-Ability, Inc.
Book Designer: Jen Wahi

Photo Credits: ©Dudarev Mikhail/Shutterstock.com, 5; ©Alexander Gitlits/Shutterstock.com, 7; ©NaKal2iN/
Shutterstock.com, 8; ©Ruslan Kalnitsky/Shutterstock.com, 11; ©West Coast Scapes/Shutterstock.com, 13; ©Elzbieta
Sekowska/Shutterstock.com, 14; ©John Brueske/Shutterstock.com, 17; ©pixelheadphoto digitalskillet/Shutterstock.
com, 19; ©Luis Molinero/Shutterstock.com, 21; ©Yuriy Kulik/Shutterstock.com, 23; ©Sherry Saye/Shutterstock.com,
25, ©By Barandash Karandashich/Shutterstock.com, 27; ©By Ko Backpacko/Shutterstock.com, 28; ©Andrea Danti/
Shutterstock.com, cover and interior; Various grunge/texture patterns throughout courtesy of Shutterstock.com

45th Parallel Press is an imprint of Cherry Lake Publishing.

Library of Congress Cataloging-in-Publication Data

Names: Loh-Hagan, Virginia, author.
Title: Adventure stories / by Virginia Loh-Hagan.
Description: [Ann Arbor : Cherry Lake Publishing, 2019] | Series: Stone
    circle stories. Culture and folktales | Includes bibliographical references and index.
Identifiers: LCCN 2018035174| ISBN 9781534143494 (hardcover) | ISBN
    9781534140059 (pbk.) | ISBN 9781534141254 (pdf) | ISBN 9781534142459
    (hosted ebook)
Subjects: | CYAC: Adventure and adventurers--Folklore. | Folklore.
Classification: LCC PZ8.1.L936 Adv 2019 | DDC [398.2]--dc23
LC record available at https://lccn.loc.gov/2018035174

Printed in the United States of America
Corporate Graphics

ABOUT THE AUTHOR:

Dr. Virginia Loh-Hagan is an author, university professor, and former classroom teacher. Her wildest adventure was traveling to Italy by herself for 3 weeks. Her goal was to eat lots of yummy food. She lives in San Diego with her very tall husband and very naughty dogs. To learn more about her, visit www.virginialoh.com.

TABLE OF CONTENTS

ADVENTURE STORIES

How can adventure stories be described?
What are some examples of adventure stories?

Everyone loves a good adventure story. The hero leaves a life of comfort. The hero faces dangers. The hero gets in and out of trouble. The hero saves the day. Adventure stories are fun. They're exciting. They're daring. They're packed with action. They're **fast-paced**. Fast-paced means they move quickly.

Adventure tales can include survival stories. They can include fantasy. They can include **journeys**. Journeys are trips. Adventure tales can include **quests**. Quests are trips with specific goals.

Adventures help heroes grow into better people.

People read adventure stories. They want to experience some fun without risking their lives.

CHAPTER 1

MONSTER SLAYERS

Who are the monster slayers?
What is their goal?
Where did this story come from?

The Navajo are Native Americans. They live in Arizona, Utah, and New Mexico.

They have a story they tell. Long ago, there were monsters. These monsters hid along roads. They ate travelers. Many humans died. The First Man got worried. He asked the gods for help. The gods said, "We will send you **saviors**." Saviors are people who save others from danger.

There are many stories about twins across different Native American tribes.

White Shell Woman was a goddess. She was the daughter of Earth and Sky. She had twin boys. The twins had magic. They could **slay** monsters. Slay means to kill. One twin was named Born from Water. The other twin was named Slayer of **Alien** Gods. Alien means a being not from this place.

The twins trained. They learned to fight. One day, they wanted to know who their father was. They went on an adventure. They traveled east. They met the Wind People. The twins asked, "Do you know who our father is?"

The Wind People said, "Your father is the Sun. He lives at the top of the rainbow."

The twins found the Sun. Sun said, "Prove you're my sons." He threw the twins into the mountains. He sent them to die in the heat. The twins lived.

The twins sang songs of protection.

We're the world's first superheroes!

SPOTLIGHT BIOGRAPHY

Pasang Lhamu Sherpa Akita is an adventurous woman. She has gotten many awards for her adventures. One of her awards is National Geographic's 2016 People's Choice Adventurer of the Year. Akita was born in 1984. She's from Nepal. She was one of the first women to climb the world's tallest mountains. She was one of the first women in Nepal to be a mountaineering teacher. She said, "As a child, I said I wanted to climb Mount Everest. I was told it was not a woman's job." Akita didn't let anyone stop her. She had other challenges. Both her parents died by the time she was 15 years old. She took care of her younger sister. In 2015, there was a big earthquake in Nepal. She helped many people. She said, "We have to do something for the people who are in trouble." She also started the Aayam Foundation. She helped girls get an education.

The Sun said, "You've passed my tests. You can live here and have all the riches you want."

The twins said, "We didn't come for riches. We want to kill all the monsters. We need your help."

The Sun was proud of his sons. He gave them many powers. He also made them **immune**. Immune means they can't get hurt. The Sun said, "Take these prayer sticks. Born from Water will watch the sticks. He'll protect the remaining humans. Slayer of Alien Gods will kill the monsters. If the sticks burn, Slayer of Alien Gods is in danger. Born from Water will come help."

The Sun opened the doors to the world. He let the twins travel on lightning bolts. The twins traveled east, west, north, and south. They went on many adventures. They worked together to kill all the monsters. The monsters' dead bodies formed mountains. The monster slayers saved the humans. They were the Navajos' saviors.

Today, Navajo people may wear traditional clothing to honor their history.

CHAPTER 2

KATE SHELLEY

Who was Kate Shelley?
What was her adventure?
How is she a hero?

Kate Shelley lived from 1863 to 1912. She was born in Ireland. She moved to Iowa. She's a real person from history. But many stories about her adventure are **tall tales**. Tall tales are special stories. They have true details combined with details that are not true. This retelling stays close to the true details. Retellings are new versions of a story.

On July 6, 1881, there were heavy storms. There was thunder. There was lightning. There were hard rains. This caused a flood. The flood washed out a bridge. The bridge fell. A train came. It crashed into the river. This happened around midnight. Four people were in the train.

The story takes place around the Des Moines River valley. The river flows from Minnesota to Iowa.

Shelley heard the crash. She ran over. She saw the men in the river. She couldn't reach them.

She yelled, "I'm going to get help!" She knew another train was coming. She didn't want more people to get hurt. She had to hurry.

It was dark. It was stormy. The light in Shelley's lantern blew out. She had to move in the dark. She crawled over

Kate Shelley was the oldest of five children. Her family was poor.

the broken bridge. She crawled on her hands and knees. She used flashes from the lightning to see. She cut her hands. A tree fell in front of her. It almost killed her.

Shelley didn't quit. She ran for 2 miles (3.2 kilometers) to the closest train station. She yelled, "The bridge fell! Stop the next train! Four people are stuck! Send help!"

The station manager closed the tracks. This saved over 200 people.

FAST-FORWARD TO MODERN TIMES

Today, there are many stories about Bigfoot. Bigfoot is an ape-like monster. He's over 10 feet (3 meters) tall. He's hairy. There are over 6,000 Bigfoot sightings in North America. Native Americans told stories about "hairy giants." J. W. Burns collected these stories. He did this in the 1920s. He first used the word "sasquatch." Jerry Crew found a 16-inch (40.6 centimeters) footprint. This happened in 1958. This happened in Bluff Creek, California. The newspapers called the creature Bigfoot. The name stuck. Crew's footprint was fake. His boss tricked him. But it didn't matter. The legend of Bigfoot started. People go on wild adventures to find Bigfoot. They travel around the world. They report sightings. They take photos. They film their journeys. They find footprints. They find hair. Some evidence may be real. Some is fake. But people want to believe. BFRO is the Bigfoot Field Researchers Organization. It collects information about people's Bigfoot adventures.

Shelley brought back a **rescue** group. Rescue means to save. The first man was in a tree. Shelley threw a rope to him. She pulled him to safety. The second man was trapped until the flood died down. He was saved after the storms. The third man died. His body was found a few days later. The fourth man was never found.

Someone asked her, "How did you know what to do?"

Shelley said, "My father and brother died in that river. They both worked for the railroad. That river owes me a favor or two."

Shelley became a hero at age 15. People wrote poems about her. They sent her money. They sent her gifts. Shelley got a job as the station manager.

Kate Shelley was the first woman in the United States to have a bridge named after her.

CHAPTER 3

TWO TRAVELERS AND A FARMER

What was the goal of the two travelers?
What did the farmer tell them?
What is the lesson of this story?

There was a traveler. He wanted an adventure. He wanted to see the world. He wanted to find the most interesting place. He walked by a farm. He saw a farmer. He said, "Hello, Farmer!"

The farmer was working on his land. He stopped. He saw the traveler. He said, "Hello, Traveler!

This story is an American parable. Parables are short stories that teach lessons.

The traveler asked, "What sort of people live in the next town?"

The farmer answered, "What sort of people are you looking for?"

The traveler said, "I want to have some fun. I want to meet people who like to party. I want to meet people who tell interesting stories."

CROSS-CULTURAL CONNECTION

"Little Peachling" is a Japanese folktale. Hundreds of years ago, there lived an old man and his wife. One morning, the woman went to the river. She was washing dishes. She saw a peach floating. She took it home. She gave it to her husband. Just before the man took a bite, the peach split in two. Out popped a little baby. The man and woman raised the baby. They named him "Little Peachling." Little Peachling grew strong and brave. He said, "I'm going to the monsters' island. I'm going to take their riches. I'll need dumplings for my journey." His parents made him dumplings. He left. He met a monkey. He met a bird. He met a dog. He gave them dumplings to join him. He and his new friends fought the monsters. They captured the king. They took the riches. Everyone lived happily ever after. The lesson is all good deeds are rewarded.

The farmer said, "Well, you're in luck. That's exactly what you'll find in the next town."

The traveler said, "That makes me so happy. Thank you!" He continued on his way.

The farmer went back to work. But then, another traveler came by. She'd been traveling for weeks. She was tired. She wanted to rest her feet. She saw the farmer. She said, "Hello, Farmer!"

The farmer said, "Hello, Traveler!"

The traveler asked, "What are the people in the next town like?"

Some people say the lesson is about how our outlook on things determines our experience.

The farmer answered, "How would you like them to be?"

The traveler said, "I'd like them to be calm. I want some peace and quiet."

The farmer said, "Lucky you! The next town is the best place for you."

The traveler said, "That's great news. Thank you!" She walked toward the town.

The farmer went home. His wife asked him, "Did anything interesting happen today?"

The farmer said, "I met two travelers. They asked me about the next town. I told them what they wanted to hear."

The wife said, "No one has lived in that town for years."

The farmer said, "Maybe they'll meet each other."

Some adventure stories are about travelers who just travel. They don't have plans for a final destination.

CHAPTER 4

STAGGER LEE

Who is Stagger Lee?
What are some of his adventures?
What happened to him?

Stagger Lee has several names. He's known as Stack Lee and Stagolee. He's a character from African American tall tales. He was an odd baby. He was born with a full set of teeth. He was born with a mask over his face. His mother called for a **fortune teller**. Fortune tellers can see the future. The fortune teller said, "This baby will come to no good."

Stagger Lee grew up in Georgia. He didn't want to pick cotton. Back then, that was the only job he would have.

Stagger Lee is based on Lee Shelton.

He ran away at age 2. He made money by playing his guitar. He also made money by playing cards. He traveled to the north. He had many adventures. He met many people.

Stagger Lee settled in St. Louis, Missouri. One day, the devil came. He said, "Stagger Lee, I'll make you a deal.

I'll give you this magical cowboy hat. You have to give me your soul."

Stagger Lee loved hats. But he wasn't sure. He asked, "What makes that hat so special?"

The devil said, "It's made from a panther that eats men. If you wear this hat, you'll have magical powers. You can crawl into bottles. You can turn into a horse and run away. You can change into mountains. You can eat hot fire. You'll never be beat."

Stagger Lee loved playing card games. He hated losing. He said, "Devil, you've got a deal."

One night, Stagger Lee was playing cards. He was winning. He took his hat off. He hung it on his chair. The devil saw his chance. He changed into a man named

Stagger Lee and the devil are known as tricksters.

Billy Lyons. He took Stagger Lee's hat. Stagger Lee got mad. He found the real Billy Lyons. He thought that Billy Lyons took his hat. He killed him.

The devil laughed. He had tricked Stagger Lee. Stagger Lee was jailed for 75 years. When Stagger Lee died, the devil took his soul. Stagger Lee was forced to amuse the devil. He played guitar in a jazz band. He did this forever.

There are songs about Stagger Lee and Billy Lyons.

DID YOU KNOW?

➤ Some people have ADHD. ADHD is attention deficit/hyperactivity disorder. This makes it hard for them to focus. They have a hard time controlling behaviors. Scientists found that people with ADHD like risks. They like exciting activities. They like adventures.

➤ Adrenaline is a chemical. It's made by the body in times of stress. It gives people the energy to flee or fight. It helps people live through adventures.

➤ James Asquith is British. He set a world record. He's the youngest man to travel to every country in the world. He visited 196 countries by age 24. He started traveling at age 16. He started in Southeast Asia. He ended his trip in Micronesia. He said, "I thought, 'I want to see more,' and eventually decided I wanted to go everywhere."

CHALLENGE:

WRITE YOUR OWN TALE

BEFORE YOU WRITE:

- Read more adventure tales. Use them as models. Notice how heroes act and react to danger.
- Make a list of adventures. Think of things you'd like to do yourself. Think of things you'd never do.
- Do research about your adventure topic. For example, if your hero is going to sea, learn more about sea travel.
- Create a hero. Make a list of strengths. Make a list of weaknesses.
- Consider adding sidekicks. Sidekicks are helpers. Heroes need help. They need friends.
- Create villains. Villains are the bad guys. They fight against heroes. They cause problems for heroes.

AS YOU WRITE:

- Describe the quest or mission. Explain the hero's goal. A goal could be to survive.
- Describe the hero's adventures. Describe exciting events.
- Increase suspense. Make sure the hero is out of his or her comfort zone. The unknown is very scary.
- Include dangers and risks. Make sure events are not ordinary. Make sure the hero is always in and out of dangers. Make sure each danger is more dangerous than the last one.
- Include surprises. Keep readers on their toes.
- Describe how the hero is rewarded.

AFTER YOU WRITE:

- Proofread and edit your adventure tale.
- Add details to keep the story interesting and exciting.
- Cut details to make sure the story moves quickly and has lots of action. Spend more time on the hero's actions. Don't spend a lot of time describing characters. Adventure heroes do more acting than thinking.
- Create a fun title.
- Share the story with others.
- Consider making a video promoting your story.

CONSIDER THIS!

TAKE A POSITION! Do you like reading or watching adventure stories? Which one is better? Argue your point with reasons and evidence.

SAY WHAT? Read the 45th Parallel Press series about true survival. Explain how these are adventure stories. Explain the dangers. Explain how people overcame the dangers.

THINK ABOUT IT! Some people are more daring. They're more likely to take risks. They like danger. Why are some people more adventurous than others? How adventurous are you? What makes you think so?

LEARN MORE!

Amin, Karima. *The Adventures of Brer Rabbit and Friends: From the Stories Collected by Joel Chandler Harris.* New York: DK, 2006.

Randolph, Joanne (ed.). *Early American Legends and Folktales.* New York: Cavendish Square Publishing, 2018.

Yolen, Jane. *Once There Was a Story: Tales from Around the World, Perfect for Sharing.* New York: Simon & Schuster Books for Young Readers, 2017.

GLOSSARY

alien (AY-lee-uhn) a being from another world or place

fast-paced (FAST PASED) a story that moves quickly because there's lots of action

fortune teller (FOR-chuhn TEL-ur) a person who sees the future

immune (ih-MYOON) not able to be hurt or harmed

journeys (JUR-neez) trips

quests (KWESTS) trips with specific goals

rescue (RES-kyoo) the act of saving people in danger

saviors (SAYV-yurz) people who save others from danger

slay (SLAY) to kill

tall tale (TAWL TAYL) story that has both true and exaggerated details

INDEX